Any Fool Can Start A War

**a play by Stan's Cafe
with Billesley Primary School**

ISBN 978-1-913185-07-7

Published by Stan's Cafe
Birmingham, UK
2020

www.stanscafe.co.uk

Any Fool Can Start A War © Stan's Cafe 2013
Photos © Graeme Braidwood 2013
Lyrics © Luke Deane & Billesley Primary School 2013
Publication © Stan's Cafe 2020

Contents:

Any Fool Can Start A War   1
Bonus Material
Original programme notes   46
Article for research in drama education   50

Act 1

Scene 1: **Bed Time**
[Illustrations drawn by students are projected as backdrops locating every scene]
[A bedroom in Billesley, Emma is trying to sleep]

Emma: Mum, I'm worried.
Parent: Why? What about? You've got nothing to worry about.
Emma: I'm worried about school tomorrow; I've had some trouble.
Parent: With a teacher? The children? With the work?
Emma: There are some children, I'm afraid they're going to beat me up.
Parent: Why do you think that? Have they said so?
Emma: No, but they look at me funny.
Parent: "Look at you funny?" But you don't know what they're thinking do you? Maybe you should talk to them. It might not be as bad as you think.
Emma: Mmm… maybe.
Parent: Well try not to worry about it now. It will all seem better in the morning.
Emma: I won't be able to sleep.
Parent: Would it help if I told you a story?
Emma: Yes please.
Parent: Okay then, settle down, close your eyes and relax.
[History animation projected with parent's voice recorded as narration]
Recording: Once upon a time, a long, long time ago, even before your parents were born, there was a war. The war had been very long and very bloody. It lasted so long, spread so wide and involved so many people that it was called the World War and one of the tragic things about this war was that it wasn't the first World War, it was the second and it only ended when one side invented a bomb so powerful it could destroy a city.

The enemy's capital city was captured, but the winners argued. The red winners believed in one way of living and the blue winners believed in another. They argued so much that these allies now became enemies and the city they had captured together now had a giant wall built right across its middle, splitting it into a blue half and a red half.

The new enemies, who had once been friends, continued to argue and they argued so much that they raced to be the first to blast dogs and humans into space and they raced to build the biggest bombs. Soon their bombs were many times stronger than those that had ended the Second World War and soon they realised that between them they had so many bombs that if they were to fight a Third World War then no one on earth would survive.

Parent: Okay, that's enough for tonight. Sweet dreams.
[Parent leaves. Emma stays in bed, which becomes a table in the Kremlin]

Scene 2: Soviet Missile Map
[The Kremlin]

Gromyko: Comrade Khrushchev, things seem peaceful now but we are worried, the Americans have so many nuclear missiles pointing at us from so many different angles.

Aide 2: They're installing these new Minutemen missiles across their country with solid fuel; they can be launched faster than any of ours.

Gromyko: They have nuclear weapons right across Europe too. They have Thor missiles in England and Jupiter missiles in both Italy and Turkey.

Aide 2: Turkey Comrade! They're in our backyard now and these monsters are far more powerful than the Little Boy and Fat Man that destroyed those Japanese cities.

Khrushchev: *[Aside]* Fat Man? Little Boy?

Aide 3:	Names of the bombs comrade.
Gromyko:	If they press The Button comrade the Union of Soviet Socialist Republics is gone. Wiped out.
Aide 2:	Obliterated!
Aide 3:	I'm really worried he's going to punch us in the face tomorrow sir.
Khrushchev:	He's young. He's ill. He's a posh boy. We can find a way to get to him. We can push him around.

Scene 3: **US Early Worries**
[The White House]

RFK:	Mr President, we're worried, Khrushchev pushed you around in Vienna. He didn't seem to be taking you seriously.
JFK:	I know. I'm trying to make friends and get an agreement to stop nuclear testing but he's not going for it at all. He wasn't even listening.
RFK:	I'm worried he's preparing a pre-emptive strike, Sir.
LeMay:	We've got to make sure he knows that if he punches us in the face we will smash him up much, much worse.
JFK:	Thanks General, for your advice, I'll bear that in mind. Emma, what do you think?
Emma:	Me? I… I don't know. It's difficult to say.

Scene 4: **Cuban Party**
[A restaurant in Havana]

Business:	Great party Fulgencio!
Gangster:	Credit to youz guys, youz really know how to have a good time. Da rum, da gambling, da cigars, da sugar, da copper,
Business:	We love your natural resources and liberal attitude to having a good time.
Batista:	Thank you. It's great having you here as my guests.
Manager:	Signore Presidente, please could you settle the tab? It is long overdue. I am struggling to pay my staff.

	These mojitos don't make themselves you know.
Batista:	Of course, of course. One minute.
	[Frisking himself he turns to others]
	Gentlemen, I seem to have left my wallet at home, I wonder if you could see your way to…
Gangster:	Sure…
Business:	That wallet of yours does often go missing, doesn't it Fulgencio.
Batista	You know what wallets are like…
Gangster:	Sure, never as fat as you'd like eh?
Batista:	Exactly. *[Turns to Manager]*
	Here you go my man.
Manager:	*[Counting money]* But Signore Batista, this is only half of the bill, what about the rest?
Batista:	Half is better than nothing, isn't it? If I didn't bring these rich Yankees to your club you'd not even have that. Next time I will be able to give you more.

Scene 5: **Revolution Planned**
[Emma is now sitting at the table with the revolutionaries]

Fidel: That Batista, our so-called President, he is rich and our people are poor.
Raul: He parties and drinks champagne with criminals while we have nothing, not even clean water.
Fidel: We have nothing. Cuba has nothing. He has given it all away to the Americans. They suck the life out of our beautiful home.
Raul: We give with our hard work and they take.
Che: We must do something.
Fidel: We need change.
Che: We need a revolution.
Fidel: But we are few and they are many.
Raul: But we are right and they are wrong.
Che: We must fight them.
Fidel: Build a new Cuba.
All: Revolution!
Emma: Revolution.

[The Revolutionaries storm the party. Batista, the Gangster and Exiles flee, the Manager is delighted, other workers come in to celebrate]

The Cuban Song

Refrain *[interlocking Cuban rhythms]*

Castro looks on it's a revolution x7
Castro looks ON!

We need more money
A safe and happy home
Less military action
Stand together and never
ALONE!

It's time for the test
To show are we better than the rest?
Freedom! Freedom! Freedom!

Castro looks on it's a revolution x 7
Castro looks ON!

Scene 6: **US Embargo**
[The Oval Office]

Exile 3:	Sir, It's the Cubans Sir, they have taken all our stuff.
Exile 1:	They took our cigars Sir.
Gangster:	And our casinos.
Business:	And our mines. They say it's their copper Sir, but we built the mines.
Gangster:	They nicked our stuff Sir and they won't give it back. What are you going to do about it Sir?
Exile 1:	They're communists Sir and they stole our lunch money.
Gangster:	We all hate communists Sir. You hate communists don't you Emma?
Emma:	I suppose so.
Business:	See! What are you going to do Sir?
Exile 1:	You've got to smash them up Sir!
JFK:	We'll ignore them.
All:	Ignore them!
Business:	Is that all?
JFK:	It's all you need to do. Don't buy their sugar, or copper, or tobacco don't buy anything from them.
RFK:	Oh yeah and don't sell them anything, ignore them, see how they like that, see how they manage.
Exile 3:	So you are saying, don't be friends any more?
Business:	Brilliant! We're the richest people round here, if we're not their friends then they're in real trouble.

Scene 7: **Batista And Border Guard**
[Border Control, Dominican Republic]

Guard:	Name?
Batistia:	Batista.
Guard:	FULL name?
Batista:	Fulgencio Batista y Zaldivar.
Guard:	Occupation?
Batista:	President of Cuba.
	[Look from guard] Former President of Cuba.
Guard:	Purpose of visit?
Batista:	To avoid getting shot by the revolutionaries at home.
Guard:	Welcome to the Dominican Republic.
Batista:	Thank you. *[Exit]*
Guard:	Next!

Scene 8: **Cubans Sell Sugar To Soviets**
[Outdoor Cafe, Havana]

Che:	Signore comrade, they won't buy anything from us.
Raul:	And they won't sell us anything.
Che:	What are we going to do?
Raul:	We've got no money. We're running out of medicines and all sorts and we've got all this sugar we don't know what to do with.
Manager:	One lump or thirty eight?
Alexeyev:	One will be fine, thank you. I appreciate your problem. I will have to ask Moscow but I'm sure we can supply you with medicines and anything else you need. I'm sure payment in sugar will be fine. We are happy to help out fellow comrades at any time, especially when they are being oppressed by the capitalists. We can be best friends.
Che & Raul:	Yes! High cinco! *[They high five]*

Scene 9: **Bay Of Pigs Set Up**
[The Oval Office]

LeMay: You need to send in the 101st Airborne Sir. We need to smash these guys, they're cosying right up to the Soviets Sir.

Business: With respect Sir, your embargo plan was a terrible idea, Sir.

LeMay: These guys only understand force Sir. You've got to send in the 101st Sir.

Business: The locals don't want to live in a communist country Sir, the counter-revolution is just waiting for some encouragement.

LeMay: If we kick it off Sir, they'll join us. They're just scared. If we land the first punch the others will soon pile in on our side.

JFK: Are you sure?

LeMay: Super-sure sir. Just send in the 101st Sir.

JFK: Okay, I don't want that Batista back. I don't mind helping the counter-revolution along, but I don't want to get into trouble with this. I don't want any of our boys involved.

Exile 2:	Okay, we'll do it. Give us the guns, show us how to shoot them, give us a lift over there and we'll get stuck in.
JFK:	Okay, but if you get into trouble don't expect me to come and sort it out for you. I don't know anything about this.
Exile 1:	About what?
JFK:	I don't know.
Exile 2:	Neither do I.
Exile 1:	Exactly.
JFK:	Who are you?
Exile 1:	I don't know.
Exile 2:	What are we doing here?
Exile 1:	We'll go. *[To Emma]* Are you with us? *[Emma exists with Exiles]*
JFK:	What's next?

[Exiles attempt to storm Cuban territory but fail]

Scene 10: Nukes Agreed For Cuba
[Soviet HQ, Havana]

Alexeyev:	Tanks, airplanes, anti-aircraft guns, machine guns, grenade launchers: it's an impressive shopping list.
Fidel:	We've got a lot of sugar and copper we could exchange, but we thought maybe you would be willing to give us these things to secure the revolution.
Che:	It's serious now signor comrade. We fought them off this time.
Raul:	The capitalist swine ran squealing from the Bay of Pigs after we fried their bacon.
Che:	Exactly, but next time they'll come back with their mates and they're proper big boys and girls, we don't stand a chance.
Fidel:	We're the only communists this side of the Atlantic comrade and it's lonely. We're less than 100 miles from Florida comrade. Miami is 30 minutes flying time away. We're in striking distance of Washington

	and New York. It's lonely out here trying to fight them off with pistols and spades comrade.
Che:	You call us 'comrades' comrade but we see no evidence of that when it comes to fighting off the capitalist threat. We need your help.
Alexeyev:	Let us keep this list. We will see what we can do. I'm sure something will be possible.

Scene 11: **Bay Of Pigs Fall Out. Plans To Assassinate Castro**
[The Oval Office]

Exile 1:	If you don't mind me saying Sir, that Bay of Pigs invasion was a fiasco, those guys smashed us.
CIA Boss:	With respect Sir, that invasion plan was a terrible idea Sir.
JFK:	It wasn't my plan!
LeMay:	We should go again Sir, but this time with the 101st Airborne Sir. Overwhelm them with sheer force Sir.
Exile 1:	These guys only understand force Sir, you've got to send in the marines.
JFK:	Listen we are NOT sending in the marines OR the 101st. I am not having the United States accused of invading a neighbouring country.
RFK:	If we do that, it gives the Soviets permission to do the same in West Berlin, then we're in real trouble.
CIA Boss:	So what do we do?
LeMay:	We can't just leave Castro there sir. We've got to do something.
JFK:	So, get rid of Castro.
CIA Boss:	But how?
RFK:	Are you asking the President how to do your job?
CIA Boss:	No Sir.
RFK:	So use your imagination – get rid of Castro.
CIA Boss:	Sir, are you giving us permission to assassinate a foreign head of state?
RFK & JFK:	NO!
RFK:	We're just saying it would be very useful for us if, for whatever reason, Castro were no longer president in Cuba.

CIA Boss:	Understood Sir, a covert mission Sir, yes Sir, we'll think up a code name immediately Sir.
Exile 1:	Covert?
Emma:	Secret.
CIA Boss:	Cyclops, Spear Head, Operation Barber, Cigarillo.
Exile 1:	Operation Kill Castro.
CIA Boss:	It's a covert mission.
Emma:	It's got to be a code name!
Exile 1:	Got ya, something to throw them off the scent. I've got it! Operation Kill Kennedy!
CIA Boss:	We'll be in Miami, if you need us.
Exile 1:	*[Whilst leaving]* Do you get it? We say Kennedy but what we mean is Castro, do you see?
RFK:	That's that dealt with then!
JFK:	I want you to personally supervise those monkeys, make sure this thing happens.

Scene 12: **Cargo Ship Ordered**
[The Kremlin]

Khrushchev:	As we know, the Americans have nuclear missiles in England, in Turkey, in Italy.
Gromyko:	Yes, they have lots more bombs than us comrade. It is not fair.
Khrushchev:	Although between us we do have enough to blow up the world
Gromyko:	But it makes us look weak comrade. The bombs in Turkey are only a few miles away, practically on our doorstep. Imagine what they would say if we put bombs near them!
Khrushchev:	They wouldn't like it.
Gromyko:	No, but we would look strong. We would be saying that whatever you can do, we can do.
Khrushchev:	Yes, it would give us a lot of power over them. We could ask for anything we wanted. We could ask to have Berlin. All of it, not just a bit of it.
Gromyko:	Yes, "or else!"
Khrushchev:	Or else what?
Gromyko:	No, I mean "or else we will attack you".

Khrushchev:	But of course we wouldn't, that would be crazy. That would start a war. We wouldn't do that.
Gromyko:	They don't need to know that though. We just need them to think that we might.
Khrushchev:	But we have told them we wouldn't do anything like that. We have said that we wouldn't put missiles anywhere near them.
Gromyko:	We said that yes, but we could do it in secret.
Khrushchev:	How?
Aide 2:	Well we have a good friend in Cuba.
Aide 3:	Yes Mr. Castro is a good friend.
Khrushchev:	It is very useful to have a friend so close to the USA.
Aide 2:	Particularly one that doesn't like them.
Khrushchev:	Yes.
Gromyko:	We are already giving them weapons to defend themselves. Perhaps we could sneak in a few other things… some bigger things… Then we would have a base very close to the USA.
Khrushchev:	On their doorstep.
All Aides:	Yes comrade.
Khrushchev:	But they are not stupid. They would find out.
Gromyko:	But they are not expecting us to do it comrade because, as you said, we told them we wouldn't.
Aide 3:	So we could do it without them noticing?
Aide 2:	And by the time they have noticed it will be too late. We will have a nuclear base on Cuba.
Khrushchev:	And then?
Gromyko:	You would seem very strong comrade… both there and here at home. It would show that the Soviet Union will not be pushed around, will not live in fear of being attacked. You would appear strong and decisive.
Khrushchev:	Mmm. Yes, I like this plan. We will have to quietly talk to Mr Castro, without anyone knowing what we are talking about.
All Aides:	Yes comrade.
Khrushchev:	Can we trust him?
Aide 2:	He needs us.
Aide 3:	We are his friends.

Gromyko: I'm sure he would be very happy to help.
Khrushchev: Yes friends help each other, don't they Emma?
Emma: If they are friends, if it really is helping, if it is an okay thing to do.
[Khrushchev, Gromyko and Aides leave. Soviet Admiral picks up the phone]
Soviet Admiral: You have the ships which can transport the big tree trunks, is that right?
Finnish Sailor: *[On screen from live video relay]* Yes, the long tree trunks, of course, that is our specialism. What length were you looking for?
Soviet Admiral: About 20 metres 54 centimetres.
Finnish Sailor: That is a very precise tree length.
Soviet Admiral: Aaaah… we have very precise trees.
Finnish Sailor: No problem we can do that. When would you like it for?
Soviet Admiral: As soon as possible.
Finnish Sailor: Where is it going?
Soviet Admiral: That's no concern of yours.
Finnish Sailor: It's my ship. I want to know where it's going.
Soviet Admiral: Oh, yes of course. Well it's going… It's going to… to… The Tropics.

Finnish Sailor: Which tropics in particular?
Soviet Admiral: Listen, these are secret trees and so it's difficult to tell you where they are going but I can promise we are taking every precaution to ensure the United States Navy will not sink your ship.
Finnish Sailor: WHAT! Why would the US Navy want to sink my ship?
Soviet Admiral: No, no one's going to sink it, of course, no one wants to sink it, it's not going to get sunk! I'm sure we can find a price which will make this sound more attractive…

Scene 13: Codename Decided
[The Oval Office]

CIA Boss: It's Mongoose Sir.
JFK: What? What's mongoose?
CIA Boss: The codename Sir.
For 'The Thing'.
JFK: What thing?
CIA Boss: THE Thing Sir. *[Whispering]* The Castro thing.
JFK: Okay, brilliant. Thank you. *[CIA leaves]* Mongoose!

Act 2

Scene 14: On-Board Ship 1 (It's CUBA!)
[North Sea]

Soviet Officer: And we are heading for… CUBA!
All: Cuba!
Soviet Troop 1: Where's Cuba?
Soviet Capt: It's in the Caribbean.
Soviet Troop 2: Isn't that hot?
Soviet Troop 3: Yes it is.
Soviet Troop 1: Then what are we doing with this lot? *[Cold weather clothes]*
Soviet Officer: It was a trick.
Soviet Troop 1: Very funny.
Soviet Officer: No, a trick to trick the enemy, the Americans, the

	Yankees. They see the hats, the gloves, the skis, they think we are going to somewhere cold but we're not, we're going to Cuba.
Soviet Troop 2:	What are we going to do in Cuba?
Soviet Officer:	We are going to be tourists.
All:	*[Different exclamations]* Brilliant! Great! Fantastic!
Soviet Troop 2:	Do they have vodka?
Soviet Troop 3:	No but they've got rum and…
Soviet Officer:	But we are not really going to be tourists. That too is a trick. We are to help our Cuban comrades defend themselves against the enemy, the Americans, the Yankees. Underneath these tarpaulins there are weapons systems, bomber planes waiting to be bolted together, anti-aircraft guns, machine guns. In other ships sailing in front and behind us there are other weapons even more powerful than these.
Soviet Capt:	You can write postcards home but you must not mention where you are, what the weather is like, whom you are with or what you are doing.
Soviet Troop 1:	So what can we say?
Soviet Capt:	Say you are on holiday in Siberia with some friends.

The Soviet Song

And it's sometimes hard
To be Kruschev
And I work so hard
And I work so hard

And it's hard to say
How I got here today
So many battles fought along the way

And it's only me
Keeping peace and harmony
It's so much responsibility

Rap beat starts
How I care to rule is history
What the future holds is a mystery
It's a hard life
Just trying to survive
200 million people, to keep alive!

Scene 15: **U2s Are Commissioned**
[A US radar station]

Radar Op: Oh Sir, Sir, we have been tracking some unusual Soviet shipping traffic across the Atlantic in the last few days.

Chief of Staff: In what way is it unusual?

Radar Op: It's a lot more frequent than usual Sir, there could be some unusual classes of ship mixed in there too.

Chief of Staff: Are these military ships?

Radar Op: No, we don't think so, but it's difficult for us to tell for sure.

Chief of Staff: It's probably just Khrushchev sending more supplies for his pal Castro.

Radar Op: That's what I thought Sir, but we've been picking up sonar signals as well, we think these ships have a submarine escort.

Chief of Staff: An escort!

Radar Op: We're 90% sure sir.

Chief of Staff: Jeepers, what's on those boats?

Radar Op: It doesn't look good does it sir.

Chief of Staff: No. You guys keep tracking them and we'll call in some photo surveillance.

Radar Op: Yes sir. The U2s Sir?

Chief of Staff: That's classified information Captain.

Radar Op: Understood Sir.

Scene 17: **On Board Ship 2 (U2)**
[The deck of a Soviet transport ship is being mopped]

Soviet Troop 1: Is it still there?

Soviet Troop 2: Keep mopping.

Soviet Troop 1: I don't like having my photo taken.

Soviet Troop 2: So don't look up. Keep acting naturally. Don't look guilty.

Soviet Troop 1: I'm not guilty. Hey, I thought you were doing the starboard side.

Soviet Troop 2: I am.

Soviet Troop 1: No you're not, this is the port side. The boat left port – port is left starboard is right.
Soviet Troop 2: Okay, okay! I was born in Demidov, how am I expected to know port from starboard?

Scene 16:   Missile Sites Are Prepared
[Cuban countryside]

Foreman: Right guys we need all this undergrowth cleared away. We need stakes driving in on the four corners of a twelve metre square centred here, orientated North – South, East – West.
Worker 1:   Oh no!
Worker 2:   Twelve metres!
Worker 3:   You're joking!
Worker 1:   It's too hot for this!
Foreman: Then we need the square levelling off. So find the lowest point and take it down to that all over.
Worker 2:   Can we not just build up this corner?
Foreman: No, it's got to be very stable. We need shuttering ply a metre high right round the perimeter, all bracing and joints to be on the outside, we're filling the thing with concrete.
Worker 3:   What's going on?
Worker 1:   They're crazy.
Foreman: You've got three days, work through the night if you have to.
Worker 3:   Are we being paid for this?
Worker 1:   We must be, surely.
Worker 2:   In Pesos or Rubles?
Worker 3:   What?
Worker 2:   Look… *[Upstage the Soviet Officer in his Tourist Disguise]*
Worker 1:   Who's that? A Soviet?
Worker 2:   They say he's an advisor.
Worker 3:   Mmm, can't say I'm impressed with his advice so far.
Worker 1:   Yeah! I'd like to give him some advice.
Worker 2:   Shhh!

Worker 3:	Who are they? *[Pointing at the Soviet Soldiers who have just turned up]*
Worker 1:	Help?
Worker 2:	They're advisors too, but they look like soldiers to me.
Worker 3:	Poor guys, it looks like they had a terrible journey.
Worker 2:	Yeah, they look shot. I guess they didn't travel first class.
Worker 1:	Their clothes are well unfashionable too.
Worker 3:	I know; those boots are totally worn out.
Worker 2:	The boss is well kitted out though.
Worker 3:	Ha, they say the Soviet Union is the land of plenty.
Worker 2:	And equality.
Foreman:	Hey guys what's stopping you? Get on with it!
Worker 1:	Sure, what did you say? Eight by eight?
Foreman:	No, twelve by twelve. Look at the plan!
Worker 1:	That's what I thought he said, five by five.

Scene 18: **Mongoose Plot**
[CIA HQ Miami]

[The scene starts without words, a cook has his throat cut. The assassin adds poison to a bowl of food and threatens the waiter with a gun. The waiter takes the bowl to Castro who eats it and dies]

Exile 1:	*[Fake waiter]* Baritos Comrade?
CIA Boss:	*[Fake Castro]* Gracias. Eugh! *[retches and collapses]* So, is that workable?
Exile 2:	*[Assassin]* I don't know.
Exile 1:	It could work couldn't it?
Exile 2:	We'd need someone who can get close to Castro at dinnertime with poison and a gun.
Exile 1:	And we'd need the waiter to be cool with it. I could have winked at him or something.
CIA Boss:	Why would you wink?
Exile 1:	To warn him, you know…
CIA Boss:	You'd be better off whispering…
Exile 2:	I'd have shot him if he whispered.
Exile 1:	If you'd have shot me then why not just shoot Castro, then we wouldn't need to worry about all this poisoning business?
Exile 2:	Because if I'd shot him I'd have got caught. This way I can sneak away.
CIA Boss:	Pedro, what do you think?
Exile 2:	Pedro?
Exile 1:	*[To Exile 2 who is still playing dead]* Pedro! What have you done to him?
Exile 2:	Nothing! Pedro, are you OK?
Exile 3	*[Fake Cook]* Aaaah got you there!
CIA Boss:	Come on guys this is serious!
Exile 3:	We invite him to tea. We have the teapot. We pour our tea first, then his. We all drink. It's fine. He relaxes. We slip poison into the pot and pour him a refill but we don't pour ourselves a refill.
Exile 2:	Why not?
Exile 1:	Because we're not thirsty?
Exile 3:	Because there's poison in the teapot!

CIA Boss:	There's no way you're getting to drink with him.
Exile 2:	Right, we follow him round the supermarket and when he's not looking, swap his headache tablets for poison tablets in his trolley.
CIA Boss:	Do we know he gets headaches?
Exile 1:	Exploding cigars. BOOM!
Exile 3:	An exploding hat. BOOM!
Exile 2:	We give him a box with an alligator in it, wrapped up, as a birthday present.
Exile 1:	When's his birthday?
CIA Boss:	August 13th.
Exile 3:	The alligator's going to go crazy in that box.
Exile 2:	We sedate it and then put it in the box.
Exile 1:	Trip him up OUCH!
Exile 3:	Push him off a cliff AAAAH!
Exile 1:	We put a bomb under his car BOOM!
Exile 2:	We use a grenade launcher. ZAAA-BOOM! Could we get a helicopter over there?
CIA Boss:	Sure.
Exile 1:	We use a sniper with a silencer and telescopic sights hidden in a bush, a tree, on the roof of tall building. PLOP.
Others:	Plop?
Exile 3:	We suffocate him with a plastic bag.
Exile 1 & 2:	*[Laugh]*
Exile 3:	What? They are dangerous!
CIA Boss:	Okay. Let's think about this logically. What is Castro's favourite thing?
Exile 1:	His country?
Exile 2:	His cigars?
Exile 3:	His hat?
CIA Boss:	Wrong, wrong, wrong. It's his beard.
Exiles 2 & 3:	What?
Exile 1:	*[Nods agreement]*
CIA Boss:	He loves that beard, he's been growing it for years. All those revolutionary guys have beards but his is way better than the others, it earns him respect.
Exile 2:	No way!
Exile 3:	You're crazy!

CIA Boss:	Okay, two brothers. Raul and Fidel – which has the best beard?
Exile 1:	Fidel, easy.
CIA Boss:	Who's president?
Exile 1,2,3:	Fidel!
CIA Boss:	Exactly. Kill the beard – kill the man.
Exile 2,3:	What?
CIA Boss:	He loses that beard he loses his power.
Exiles 1:	Brilliant, we're on it, come on Emma! *[They exit]*
CIA Boss:	What we really need is to get the Cuban people to turn against Castro.
Exile 3:	You could drop leaflets from airplanes, telling them how much better they'd be without him. Maybe?
Exile 2:	Say, Jesse, what you say, you and I just go in there with a knapsack full of dynamite, some duck-tape and take out a copper-mine or something?
	It's ain't gonna kill Castro but it's gonna make his life tough. We do that, we do this, we do something else, before you knows it the country's gonna collapse an' they welcome us in to fix it all back up!
Exile 3:	Wow!
Exile 2:	Whaddaya say?
Exile 3:	I'm in.
CIA Boss:	Great. We'll build you a fake copper mine...
	To practice on.
	[The others turn to him in disbelief]
CIA Boss:	Honestly we will!

Scene 19: **Missiles Are Spotted**
[Situation Room]

Carter:	Sir, we have some photographs for you, taken on Sunday Sir, over Cuba. There's a missile launch site Sir and military camps.
JFK:	Where?
Carter:	Those three dots sir. Have you got the big pictures?
Aide 1:	Yessir.
Carter:	The President would like to see those.
Aide 1:	Yessir. The big pictures.

Carter:	There are at least fourteen canvas covered missile trucks Sir, at one of the encampments. At the others are tents and vehicles and several buildings.
Aide 2:	Some buildings are being built Sir.
Aide 1:	These are the launchers Sir, for the missiles.
Carter:	The missile truck is backing up to one of them Sir.
JFK:	How do you know this is a missile?
Aide 1:	The length Sir.
JFK:	The length?
Aide 1:	Yessir.
Aide 2:	We have some pictures Sir of the same kind of missile from a parade in Moscow.
JFK:	Is this ready to be fired?
Aide 2:	No Sir.
JFK:	How long until it is, do we know?
Aide 2:	That depends Sir.
McNamara:	Could you say if there are nuclear warheads for the missiles?
Aide 1:	We've looked very hard but we/
McNamara:	I can't see any fences – would the Soviets really put nuclear bombs on a piece of ground without a fence?
Carter:	Why would there be missiles if there weren't nuclear warheads to go with them?
McNamara:	I'm sure they are nuclear but are they ready to fire? It seems to me, Mr President, that they are not ready to be fired.
Aide 1:	That doesn't mean they couldn't be fired very quickly.
McNamara:	The time between now and when they are ready to be fired is very important.
JFK:	Get Dobrynin in here, we need to know what's going on.
Aide 2:	Sir. *[Rushes off]*

Scene 20: Soviet Missiles Are Deployed
[Castro's HQ in Havana]

Commander 1:	We have R12 missile sites set up here and here, Comrade President.
Castro:	What's their range?

Commander 1:	A thousand miles.
Castro:	From here, we can hit Miami, we can hit Washington and maybe if we are very lucky, Philadelphia. Move them north, to here or here and New York comes within range. The Statue of Liberty? Ha, what liberty is that? The liberty tp invade emerging socialist republics committed/
Commander 1:	An… an… an excellent idea Comrade President we will look into the logistics of moving a battalion up to the Northern Region immediately.
Commander 2:	Meanwhile we have a battalion moving down toward Guantanamo Bay as we speak.
Castro:	Excellent! To have the aggressors camped on our island is intolerable, we must/
Raul:	Will this battalion be nuclear enabled?
Commander 2:	Yes Comrade, they will have more than sufficient firepower to obliterate the base at a stroke.
Commander 1:	We also have nuclear capability at a battlefield level. Any Yankee invasion from sea or air will be walking into hell comrade.
Raul:	It won't be comfortable for us Cubans to have this war fought on our soil/
Castro:	in defence of freedom all sacrifices are noble. Do they know we hold this threat?
Commander 1:	Who knows what they know comrade? They know it's a possibility, they suspect some of this, but probably not all.
Castro:	Mmm, which is more intimidating for them; knowing, or not knowing?

Scene 21: **Kennedy Confronts Ambassador Dobrynin**
[The Whitehouse]

CoS:	Ambassador, don't pretend you don't know.
Dobrynin:	I'm sorry but I do not know. I am not a spy. I am not an expert in aerial photographs. You seem to know what these things are, why don't you tell me?
CoS:	Those are missile launchers. Those are tents hiding missiles. Those are Soviet troops. That is Cuba.

	What are all those things doing together apart from threatening our freedom?
Dobrynin:	Well, you seem very confident in yourselves but the Soviet Union is only supplying Cuba with military advisors, agricultural machinery and some weapons to defend themselves from your threats.
CoS:	We have made no threats.
Dobrynin:	The Bay of Pigs?
CoS:	That incursion, as you know, was a spontaneous action by disgruntled Cuban exiles, conducted entirely independently of any influence from the United States.
Dobrynin:	Flying pigs!
CoS:	We've been tracking shipping from Soviet ports right through the North Atlantic. You are installing nuclear weapons on Cuba. This is unacceptable in any mode, offensive or defensive.
Dobrynin:	There are no nuclear warheads in or on their way to Cuba.
CoS:	Flying pigs, Mr. Ambassador. Your guys need to know, you ship those things straight back out again or the consequences will be very strong and very direct.
Dobrynin:	The Soviet Union does not respond well to threats, Mr. Chief of Staff.
JFK:	Neither does the United States of America, Mr. Ambassador.
Dobrynin:	Mr. President. *[Exits]*
Rusk:	He was bluffing.
RFK:	It wouldn't surprise me if he had less idea what's going on in Cuba than we do.
JFK:	*[Sarcastic]* Brilliant.
Rusk:	Sir, if the ambassador's out of the loop we need better ways of getting messages to Khrushchev. We need to explore back channels.

The American Song

Don't give up now Kennedy
Don't press the button
Don't press the button
Responsibilities...

[Spoken]
JFK leads the space race
American Image
It's a test of face...

Don't give up now Kennedy
Don't press the button
Don't press the button
Responsibilities...

[Spoken]
America
The land of the brave
We'll stand through everything
Never to be slaves

[Spoken]
Kennedy knows that this is his moment...

Scene 22: **US Decides What To Do**
[The Situation Room]

JFK: *[On the phone]* No Jackie, don't worry, take the children out to Virginia… It'll be far enough… Who knows?… We'll do our best. Listen, I've got to go now. Kiss the children for me… Call from the ranch when you're there… Love you too. *[Phone down]* So we know there are Soviet bases on Cuba with missiles but we don't know if the missiles are ready to be fired at us or if they are nuclear.

Aide 2: We are sure they are though Sir.

McNamara: Probably.

Aide 1: Almost certainly.

JFK: So what do we do about it? Mr Rusk?

Rusk: Well Sir. I don't think we can sit still.

JFK: So?

Rusk: We could take some sudden action, a surprise of some kind, a quick strike… or do something slower, until the other side has to think about giving up.

JFK: Such as?

Rusk: We could get in touch with Castro, perhaps via a third party and tell him that we know what is happening so that he knows that we know.

Aide 1: Yeah, tell him.

Rusk: Tell him that the Soviets have put him in a very difficult position and that we will have to think about attacking him.

Aide 1: Yeah, tell him we'll fight him.

Aide 2: Yes, but if we tell him what we might do, he might do something to stop us doing the thing we might do.

JFK: Okay, what about the military thing?

CoS: We've been doing some more thinking. We could launch an airstrike to take out the missiles with twenty four hours warning.

Aide 2: But the military chiefs are worried that that might not be enough and then they might fight back.

CoS: So we recommend getting more information, more pictures, so we know exactly what is there and then

	take it all out with one hard crack.
JFK:	Think that could be done in one day?
CoS:	We could take out a lot in one day, but would need five days to do the whole job. Meanwhile we could think about invading the island.
McNamara:	It seems to me that any military action we take will make the Soviets take action somewhere in the world.
Aide 2:	We could be bombed in Florida Sir. That could do some damage.
JFK:	But not much.
Aide 1:	What if they used a nuclear bomb.
JFK:	We have to believe they wouldn't do that. What I don't understand is why the Soviets are doing this. They promised not to send weapons that could attack us. What if they carry on putting in more bases?
RFK:	And then, in a few years time, if there's a problem in South America that we need to deal with, Castro could say "You go down there and we'll fire our missiles".
Aide 1:	That will make us look like we are scared of Cuba and that we just sat back and let them do this.
JFK:	You could say it doesn't matter if you get hit by a bomb from ninety miles away or a thousand miles away. I shouldn't have said we wouldn't allow them to do this. Now I've said it and they've done it we can't just do nothing.
RFK:	So what do we do?
JFK:	The message to Castro doesn't seem much use. So, Option 1 – an air strike to take out the missiles. Option 2 – an air strike to take out the missiles and aircraft and other equipment. Option 3 – invade.
Emma:	Option 4 – tell a teacher.
RFK:	*[To Emma]* The United Nations are powerless in this context.
Aide 2:	The President doesn't have to make a decision about what to do until twenty four hours before an air strike.

	He just has to make a decision about preparing for an air strike.
RFK:	I think we need to talk about the consequences. What kind of world do we live in after air strikes? A small air strike could mean they attack us. A big air strike is a much bigger operation with much bigger consequences.
Aide 1:	I would say a small air strike followed by invasion.
Aide 2:	I'm against invasion.
RFK:	If we do knock out the bases what's to stop them building more?
McNamara:	Then you have to put in a blockade.
RFK:	Then you have to sink Soviet ships and Soviet submarines. Then you are getting into a war.
Aide 2:	This surprise attack scares me. It's the beginning of something not the end.

Scene 23: Khrushchev And The Blockade
[The Kremlin]

Advisor 3:	If they attack Cuba how do we respond?
Advisor 2:	We would have the only excuse needed to punch them hard in the belly and make them back down.
Gromyko:	That punch leads to a counter-punch. It gets ugly fast.
Advisor 2:	We can't back down. We can't look scared. We must look strong.
Khrushchev:	But we must keep options open, open for us and them, there must never be 'no options'. I don't believe he wants a war. We can push him hard but we must also offer him an option. I will dictate a letter.

[An airplane flies low across the stage]

Scene 24: **Castro Complains About Low Flying planes**
[Soviet Embassy Havana]

Fidel: You've got the radar, you've got the anti-aircraft guns. You've got the surface-to-air missiles for the love of Lenin! But we just stand and wave our fists at these yankee planes? Nothing more than that!

Alexeyev: I know.

Raul: These new planes, they fly so low! They scare our children, our animals and all we do is wave our fists? They are laughing at us.

Fidel: Today they may be taking photographs, in the next forty eight hours they will be dropping bombs or marines. Unless you do something about it, it will be your fault and Signor Comrade Khrushchev will/

Alexeyev: I am in constant contact with Comrade Khrushchev and he says/

Fidel: I don't care what he says. You tell him, from me, we need the radar on now, we need the guns loaded and we need those planes out of our airspace.
[Fidel and Raul exit]

Che: It is humiliating. You must persuade Khrushchev to let us fight.

Alexeyev: I will pass your thoughts on to him.

Scene 25: **Television Broadcasts**
[TV studio, live feed from camera onto screen]

TV Director: You're looking good Mr. President and we're going to you live across the nation in 5…4…3…
[Silent signals... 2… 1… points]

JFK: Good evening, my fellow citizens.
This government as promised, has maintained the closest surveillance of the Soviet military build-up on the island of Cuba. Within the past week, unmistakable evidence has established the fact that a series of offensive missile sites are now in preparation on that imprisoned island. The purpose of these bases can be none other than to provide a nuclear strike capability against the western hemisphere.
On receiving the first, preliminary, hard information of this nature last Tuesday morning…
[Video feeds cross-fade]

BBC Pres 1: … the Nuclear Clock is re-set again. It now stands at to a minute to midnight. Cuba lies isolated from the World, trembling, waiting to see if the United States of America will invade, launch an air assault or continue to try and throttle a compromise from the regime of Fidel Castro and his Soviet backers.
[Video feeds cross-fade]

BBC Pres 2: Meanwhile, John F Kennedy, the American President, has suspended his campaigning for the forthcoming mid-term elections in order to focus on this, the most dramatic crisis of his brief presidency. He must calculate the next move in this game of global chess, in which the stakes could not be higher.
[Video feeds cross-fade]

BBC Pres 1: How far is he prepared to push the Americans in his quest for nuclear supremacy? Is he prepared to take the ultimate gamble?
[Video feeds cross-fade]

BBC Pres 2: These two men with their fingers on The Button now stand eyeball to eyeball. Who will blink first? What will the consequences be? Experts say the next twenty four hours will be crucial. Around the world all we can do is look on and wait.

[Interval]

Act 3

Scene 26: **Sailing Towards Quarantine**
[Ship at sea]

Soviet Captain: One hundred and fifty miles to the US quarantine line comrade. Given the serious nature of our cargo, do we have guidance on how to approach this quarantine? Do we accept it or ignore it?

Soviet Officer: This is getting very serious. Do we have reports on US naval activity up ahead? Do we have any sense of what their terms of engagement are? Are they going

	to shoot first and ask questions later? We need to get a steer from Moscow. Until then, full steam to Cuba and try to evade any interceptions.
Soviet Captain:	Very good comrade. Full steam to Cuba.

Scene 27: **Fixing Warheads**
[Cuban countryside. A rocket is towed]

Dmitri:	Okay, back, back, back, back, slowly, SLOWLY! Left hand down. LEFT HAND! Stop stop stop!
Sergei:	What? What's your problem Dmitri?
Dmitri:	My problem is that THIS, is a two megaton warhead and YOU are a terrible driver, who doesn't know his left from his right.
Sergei:	I do!
Dmitri:	It's midnight, the temperature is STILL twenty three degrees and this thing is supposed to be kept in a stable, air-conditioned environment, NOT some farmer's shed they moved the cows out of yesterday! THIS is one of the most dangerous weapons in history and there's not a shred of barbed wire round this site.
Sergei:	There is!
Dmitri:	If the Yankees spot we're here we're dead and if you keep going the way you are we're dead sooner than that! Get back up there. Back that thing up and let's see if we can bolt it onto a missile.
Sergei:	Sure…

Scene 27: **A Cuban Officer Addressing Troops**
[Same location at night]

Cuban Officer:	My brave soldiers, this is a most important moment in our history. We are about to be invaded by the imperialist USA. It could be today, it could be tomorrow, but it is coming and we must be ready. Are you ready?
Cuban Troop 1:	I am ready!
Cuban Troop 2:	I am ready!

Cuban Troop 3: I am ready!
Cuban Officer: They have invaded our airspace. They have blockaded our seas and now they are coming for us.
Cuban Troop 2: We will not let them in!
Cuban Troop 3: Cuba is ours!
Cuban Officer: Our Soviet Socialist brothers have said that they are negotiating for peace. We can trust them, but we dare not trust the American leaders. We must protect ourselves. We must be alert.
Cuban Troops: We are ready.
Cuban Officer: If you see an American plane in the sky I want you to shoot it down. It is not American sky, it is our beautiful sky over our beautiful land. Whose sky is it?
Cuban Troop 2: It is our sky!
Cuban Troop 3: We will protect it comrade. You can trust us.
Cuban Officer: Thank you my brothers and sisters. Our future is in your steady hands and steely eyes. Good luck.
[Cuban Officer exits]
Cuban Troop 2: What's that?
Cuban Troop 3: What?
Cuban Troop 2: That noise?
Cuban Troop 3: I can't hear anything…
Cuban Troop 2: I'm scared.
Cuban Troop 3: We'll be alright. If we stick together we'll beat the bullies.
Cuban Troop 1: Together.

Scene 28: **To The Brink**
[Anderson and Maultsby are on video, various others are on mic. as a U2 is flying over the Arctic]

Maultsby: Permission to take off Sir?
US Traffic: Charlie Mike you are cleared for take off.
Maultsby: Thank you Hank. See you in eight hours.
US Traffic: Mind you don't fall asleep.
Maultsby: Yeah, midnight over the North Pole at seventy thousand feet feet, navigating by the stars, jammed in this thing, way too boring. Get me to Cuba for some proper action!

	[Video feeds cross-fade to U2 over Cuba]
Anderson:	Permission to take-off.
US Traffic:	Roger, Romeo Alpha you are cleared for take-off.
Anderson:	Thank you controller.
US Traffic:	Romeo Alpha, we have reports of Soviet radar operational over Cuba, be careful up there.
Anderson:	Thank you controller, I'm going to fly high and silent, with luck they'll never know I'm there.
US Traffic:	Sure thing, we look forward to seeing your holiday snaps, good luck!
Anderson:	A-okay going to radio silence. Speak to you in ninety minutes.
	[Video feeds cross-fade]
Maultsby:	Hank. Are you there?
US Traffic:	I'm here. I'm going nowhere. Where are you?
Maultsby:	I don't know. I'm looking for Orion directly ahead but the Aurora Borealis has wiped out all the stars, I can't recognise anything up here.
US Traffic:	You're beyond our radar but we'll keep looking.
Maultsby:	I'd appreciate that. I'm a bit worried about fuel and I'm going to have to go easy on the radio too. The batteries don't look too strong.
	[Video feeds cross-fade]

SAM Control:	Report if you get anything.
Radar Op:	Nothing interesting, low level and slow outside our territory, travelling away.
Anderson:	*[To self]* Good. That's good. Flight plan. Turn one hundred and thirty degrees left. Keep her at seventy thousand.
Radar Op:	We've got something comrade, very high but it's definitely interesting, a U2 probably, just turned up the east coast.
Anderson:	*[Buzzer buzzes]* Oh no, they've found me!
Sov General:	Spying, preparations for a bombing raid. Designate that Target Number 33. Keep tracking it.
Radar Op:	You can rely on us. Target 33 is being tracked.
SAM Control:	We've got him too now. He's ours if we want him.
Anderson:	Let's hope they're feeling friendly.
Sov General:	General Gretchko says it's time to fight back.
Anderson:	Throw out some chaff, let's get this last photo and turn for home.
SAM Control:	He's ours if we want him Comrade.
Sov General:	Destroy Target Number 33, use two missiles.
Anderson:	Okay, home time, let's get out of here. What's tha/ *[Video screen goes to white then black]*
SAM Control:	Do we have him?
Radar Op:	I've lost him.
SAM Control:	We got him?
Radar Op:	There's no signal. I think you've got him.
SAM Control:	Yes, wonderful!
US Traffic:	We've lost him... *[Video U2 over the Arctic]*
Maultsby:	May Day! May Day! This is Charlie Mike, is there anyone there?
USSR Traffic:	Roger Charlie Mike, we read you. What are your coordinates?
Maultsby:	I don't know, I need your help. I need a bearing to get me home.
USSR Traffic:	Sure, there is no problem. Take a ninety degree turn to port and that will bring you to your home. We will send some guys up to keep you company. Follow

	them in and we will welcome you home.
Maultsby:	Thank you. *[Suspicious]* Base, can you confirm today's Q code?
USSR Traffic:	You are breaking up there a little. Ninety to port and we will be seeing you.
Maultsby:	*[Worried]* Today's Q Code please base.
USSR Traffic:	Ninety to port.
MacNamara:	Sir, we've lost a U2 over Cuba
RFK:	Lost?
MacNamara:	Shot down, we think.
JFK:	Poor guy. Did he have family?
MacNamara:	Wife and two kids. There's tell the wife's pregnant.
JFK:	Okay.
LeMay:	Now the gloves are off. We smash them right? That's our excuse. Now we have the moral high ground. Now we blast them back to the Stone Age.
	[At sea on the edge of the quarantine zone]
US Navy Capt:	This is USS Joseph P Kennedy you are approaching a quarantined territory turn around!
Cargo Capt:	*[In Polish]* What is it you're saying?
US Navy Capt:	We are an American battleship and you are approaching a no go zone. Stop.

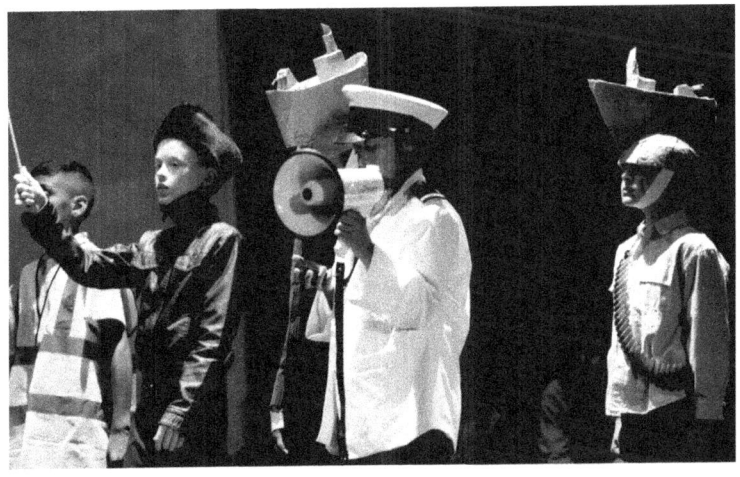

Cargo Capt:	*[In Polish]* What? I don't understand what you are saying.
US Navy Cpt:	This. Ship. Is. American. You. Must. Stop!
Cargo Capt:	*[In Polish]* Move aside, we're going to Cuba and you are right in the way!
US Navy Cpt:	Stop or we will sink you!
Cargo Capt:	*[In Polish]* What? I don't understand.
US Navy Cpt:	STOP RIGHT NOW OR WE'LL BLOW YOU OUT OF THE WATER!
	[Whitehouse Situation Room]
Aide 1:	Sir, we've lost another U2.
JFK:	What? I thought we weren't overflying Cuba any more!
Aide 1:	No, this is from Project Stardust Sir. They overfly the North Pole sampling for fallout from Soviet nuclear tests. Something has gone wrong with one of these missions, they've lost radio contact with the pilot, he's overdue and we think it highly likely that he is violating Soviet air space.
RFK:	WHAT? We're here trying to stop Khrushchev pressing the button and launching the nuclear apocalypse and one of our guys blunders over there for a cup of sugar, looking like a first strike!
LeMay:	That's it, let's do it, let's hit them as hard as we possibly can now. We hit them hard enough and they don't get up. We do that. We launch before they do and we can win this war!
JFK:	We obliterate Russia and half of Eastern Europe, bring on a nuclear winter and only lose a few million American lives in the process? That doesn't sound like a war with any winners.
RFK:	*[To aides]* We need the Soviet Ambassador in here NOW! We need him to know this is not an offensive action. They've got to know this a mistake and not World War 3.
LeMay:	Great message! We'll be toast before those goons at the embassy have got that message half way to Moscow!
Rusk:	We've just received this from Mr. Khrushchev, Sir.

JFK:	When was this written? Last Thursday! Why haven't we got a phone-line to these people? This is crazy. *[The far north eastern boarder of the USSR]*
USSR Traffic:	Comrade we've picked up an American plane penetrating our airspace.
Air Marshal:	Is this the nuclear first strike?
USSR Traffic:	We don't know, that's why we've brought it directly to you.
Air Marshal:	Okay. 1: Scramble anything we have close and get them to give us a visual. 2: Get me a projection of where it's heading, FAST. 3: Give Moscow all the information we have. 4: Keep looking at the horizon for more incoming. 5: Standby for counter-strike commands.

[The three songs together]

Scene 29: Back From The Brink

[Soviet Airspace, the Arctic Circle on video]

Maultsby:	*[Russian music]* Oh no! This really is Russia? Fuel reading… not good. Plus MIGs, this is looking very bad. Hold on… hold on… is that… sunrise! I'm going South not East. Let's swing her round ninety degrees, see if I can drop the MIGs and glide back to Alaska.

[At sea on the edge of the quarantine zone]

US Navy Cpt:	STOP RIGHT NOW OR WE'LL BLOW YOU OUT OF THE WATER!
Cargo Capt:	Okay, keep your hair on!
US Navy Cpt:	You speak English?
Cargo Capt:	And you don't speak Polish, it seems.
US Navy Cpt:	No.
Cargo Capt:	You should. It's rude to shout at people in a language they don't understand.
US Navy Cpt:	But you do understand it!
Cargo Capt:	Luckily for you.

US Navy Cpt:	Luckily for you.
Cargo Capt:	You want to sink a ship full of ammonia and start a war in the process? You're welcome.
US Navy Cpt:	We need to search your ship.
Cargo Capt:	You're welcome, but be warned, it stinks.

[Ship elsewhere at sea]

Soviet Officer:	That's confirmed, swing her around one hundred and eighty degrees, we're going home
Soviet Captain:	Hard over to Starboard, one hundred and eighty degree turn confirmed. Let's take this lot home.

[Alaska]

US Traffic:	Charlie Mike is that you Charlie Mike?
Maultsby:	*[On video]* Affirmative, it's me Hank.
Us Traffic:	Charlie Mike we're very pleased to hear from you! Head for Kotzebue Airfield and put her down as gently as you can.
Maultsby:	It's great to hear you. It's great to be in friendly air space again and it'll be great to be back on the ground again, but it'll be amazing to have a chance to go to the toilet Sir.
US Traffic:	Quite a relief?
Maultsby:	You got it.

[The Cuban countryside. A missile is being towed]

Demitri:	Okay Sergi we're packing this up.
Sergi:	What? We've only just set it up!
Demitri:	Don't blame me, orders from Moscow.
Sergi:	Are we going home then?
Demitri:	Not till this is safely on a ship and I mean safely, so take her back slowly… slowly… SLOWLY! Right hand down! Stop Stop STOP!
Sergi:	Relax Demitri… what's your problem? We're going home!
Demitri;	THIS is still a 2 megaton warhead and YOU are still a terrible driver. I am only going to relax when this is underground in a concrete bunker back in the Motherland and I am at home with Mrs Demitri.
Sergi:	I'll drink to that.

Demitri: Not while you're driving that you won't.

[The office of the President of Turkey, Cemal Gürsel]
Cemal Gürsel: Mr. McNamara, how good to see you, all the way from Washington! Please, please will you have a coffee, a sweet? What can we do for you?
McNamara: Mr. President, I have come to talk to you about our Jupiter Missiles.
Cemal Gürsel: Our Jupiter Missiles.
McNamara: I'm sorry, I should have been more precise. I've come to talk about OUR nuclear warheads that fit on the top of the Jupiter Missiles WE gave to YOU, last year. The Defence Department has decided to withdraw them from service.
Cemal Gürsel: I expected as much. This is part of some deal struck with the Soviets over that trouble you had in Cuba?
McNamara: No, no, of course not. The two things have no connection at all. The Jupiters are practically obsolete and we've been worrying about how those lightening strikes activate the thermal batteries, the tritium-deuterium leaks, none of it's good…

Scene 30: **Khrushchev Reflects**
[The Kremlin]

Gromyko: Here is the latest draft of the nuclear test ban treaty comrade.

Khrushchev: Good, where are we with the Cuban missiles?

Gromyko: All nearly home now comrade.

Khrushchev: Good. What does Castro think about that?

[Cut to Cuba]

Fidel: That traitorous hypocrite! Khrushchev promises us his support but at the first sign of trouble he's off. He abandons us!

Raul: He lacks our guts and stomach for a fight brother.

Fidel: He is a liar and a coward. He traded our security for his convenience.

Raul: We cannot rely on him, we must be self-reliant, stand up for ourselves. We must build ourselves up.

Che: We must build The Revolution. I fancy Congo or Bolivia do you want to come with me Emma?

Emma: No thanks Che, I'd rather stay here with Fidel and Raul.

Raul: Aaaah, a true friend!

Fidel: Unlike the Soviets, fair-weather friends, false revolutionaries, imperialists by any other name...

[Back to Moscow]

Gromyko It's fair to say Comrade Castro would rather we had left the missiles with him.

Khrushchev: That man is a better revolutionary than he is a politician, but he is a young man. Cuba will be fine. He will be fine. He will outlive us all, so long as he calms down and learns from this lesson.
You know Andre, any fool can start a war but once they have, even the wisest person is helpless to stop it.

Gromyko: Yes comrade.

Khrushchev: Tell your children Andre: a coward steps down, but it takes bravery to step back.

Gromyko: I will comrade, as soon as I have got home and got some sleep.

Khrushchev:	Hey you there, is that telephone wired up yet?
Emma:	Nearly there Mr. Khrushchev.
Khrushchev:	Good, good. I've been waiting so long for this… will he be there?
Emma:	He should be. Try it now comrad.
Khrushchev:	Hello… Jack?
	[Washington]
JFK:	Niki, is that really you?
Khrushchev:	It is, it is. I'm so happy to hear from you!
JFK:	It's been too long buddy!
Gromyko:	*[To RFK]* That's good to see isn't it.
RFK :	*[To Gromyko]* Isn't it.
Emma:	'Jaw jaw is always better than war war'.
	[Gromyko and RFK both look at Emma, confused]
	It's Winston Churchill, it means talking is always better than fighting.

The Telephone Song

Now you might think that this story
Doesn't have a happy ending
But the telephone to Moscow
Has a ring that's never ending

Don't run away
Stay and talk to me
Coz it's the measure of endeavour
That's at the heart of the word "free"

Three different places
One is the USA
Meetings at the White House
And the President's JFK

Another of the three is Cuba
Lying in the middle of the sea
They're having a revolution
To set their people free

The last is the USSR
And Kruschev's in the cold
It's not a game and he knows the name
Of the country he's trying to hold

Don't run away
Stay and talk to me
Coz it's the measure of endeavour
That's at the heart of the word "free"

These three got into a tussle
About who had more muscle!
Who would come out top
In the great world power re-shuffle

With no way to talk
And no way to plan
The world didn't make a sound
Everyone held their breath...

Don't run away
Stay and talk to me
Coz it's the measure of endeavour
That's at the heart of the word "free"

The finger was on the button
And the whole world was about to explode
But then they had this meeting
Discussed and decided no

Scene 31: **The Morning**
[A bedroom in Billesley]

Parent: Emma, wake up, it's time to get up.
Emma: What, already? Oh, I've been having the most crazy dream. It was about a country called Cuba and there were exploding cigars and missiles pretending to be trees and soldiers disguised as tourists and airplanes that take photographs and the whole world could have blown up at any moment just because two people didn't have a telephone!
Parent: Emma, that wasn't a dream, that was history. Everything you saw while you were asleep was true *[To the audience]* more or less.
How are you feeling about school today?
Emma: *[Confident]* School? That's not going to be a problem now. I've got strategies. Any fool can start a war mum, but I'm no fool.

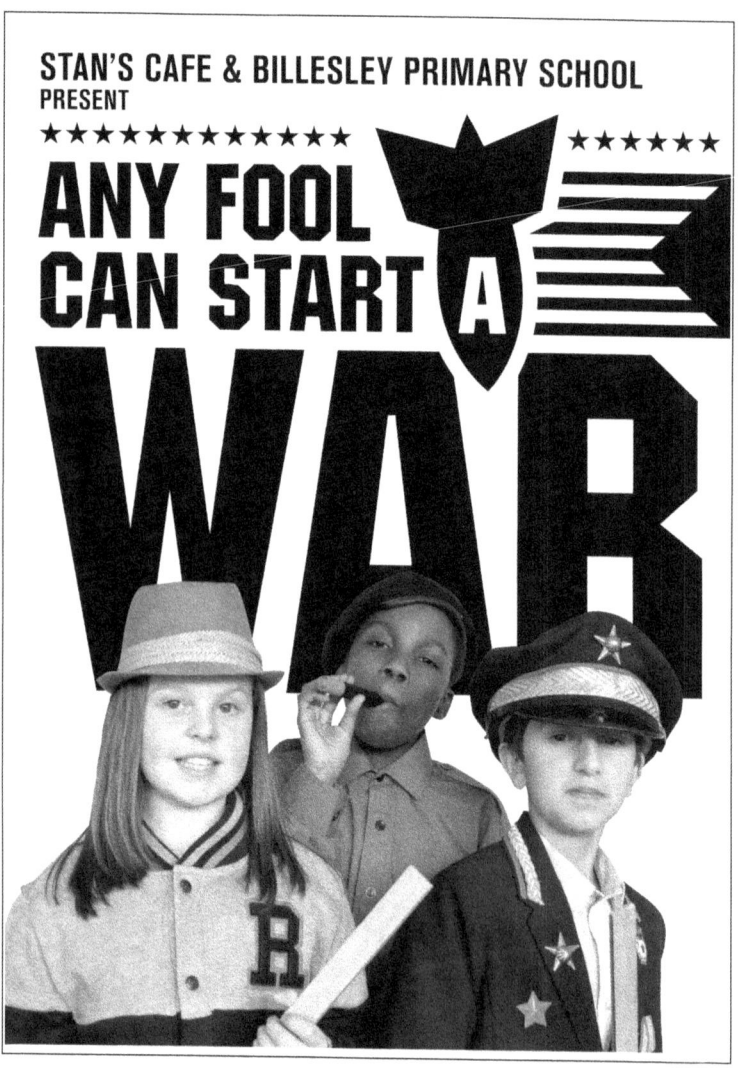

CUBANS

Fidel Castro (Revolutionary/President)	De'jaun
Raúl Castro (Revolutionary)	Saleha
Ernesto (Che) Guevara (Revolutionary)	Usman
Fulgencio Batista (President/Exile)	Salam
Cesar Garcia (Restaurant Manger)	Isobel
Eugenio Rolando Martinez (Exile)	Waqas
Miguel Orozco (Exile)	Rimshah
Pedro Vera (Exile)	Millie
Humberto Sori Marin (Revolutionary Soldier)	Hassan
Rene Ramos Latour (Revolutionary Soldier)	Nadia
Eloy Menoyo (Revolutionary Soldier)	Netsanet
Juan Almeida Bosque (Revolutionary Officer)	Freya
Emiliano Fuentes (Foreman)	Sohaib
Juan Perez (Worker)	Jamie
Jose Valdes (Worker)	Zohaib
Antonio Manuel (Worker)	Josh
Luis Martinez (Worker)	Adnan

SOVIETS

Nikita Khrushchev (First Secretary of the Communist Party of the Soviet Union)	Rumman
Andrei Gromyko (Minister of Foreign Affairs)	Sham
Marshal Georgi Zhukov (Minister of Defence)	Abubakar
Mikhail Suslov (Chairman of the Foreign Affairs Commission)	Malachi
Alexandr Alexevey (Ambassador to Cuba)	Kieran
Demitri Kaverin (Military Engineer)	Easah
Sergei Terekhov (Military Driver)	Jay
A A Dementyev (Commander of Soviet Military Mission in Cuba)	Ethan
Pavel Nasonov (Soviet Officer)	Hashaam
Viktor Mikheev (Solider)	Abdullah
Vadim Orlov (Soldier)	Moin
Maxim Leskov (Soldier)	Owen
Leonid Ivanovich Sannikov (Commander)	Ali A
Dmitry Timofeevich Yazov (Commander)	Wail
Anatoly Dobrynin (Ambassador to USA)	Reiss
Stepan Kadnikov (Radar Operator)	Aaron
Bogdan Abramov (SAM Control)	Danyal
Anton Babkin (Soviet General)	Ali R
Ivan Dyogtin (Soviet Admiral)	Easah
Igor Kandinsky (Airtraffic Control)	Tayyab
Konstantin Andreevich Vershinin (Air Marshal)	Chris

AMERICANS

Herb Kilmer (Business Man)	Alishba
John Roselli (Gangster)	Ellie
John Fitzgerald Kennedy (President)	Shannon
Robert Francis Kennedy (Attorney General)	Courtney
Curtis LeMay (Airforce General)	Irtiqa
John McCone (Director of the CIA)	Almas
Robert McNamara (Secretary of Defence)	Ayza
Marshall Carter (Deputy CIA Director)	Chitra
Clark Clifford (National Security Advisor)	Alisha
George Bundy (National Security Advisor)	Lauren
General Maxwell D Taylor (Chief of Staff)	Amani
Dean Rusk (Secretary of State)	Jasmine
Nicholas S. Mikhalevsky (Navy Captain)	Liberty
Rudolf Anderson (U2 Pilot)	Lauren
Charles W Maultsby (U2 Pilot)	Hollie
Hank Roberts (Radar Operator)	Evelyn

OTHERS

Bernard Peters (TV Director)	Chloe
Jenny Jennings (BBC Announcer)	Kayleigh
Michael Charlton (BBC Announcer)	Reiss
Miroslav Havel (Polish Ship Captain)	Dawid
Cemal Gürsel (President of Turkey)	Daanyal
Mirtha Montez (Boarder Control Guard)	Nicholia
Jesse Jokelainen (Finnish Sailor)	Jessica
Child	Emma
Parent	Miss Zielinska

Written by: James Yarker and Craig Stephens with Year 6

Film by: George Flemming, Keith Bloomfield and Year 6

Music by: Luke Dean and Christine Cornwell

Songs by: Year 6 with Luke Deane

Costumes by: Kay Wilton

Design by: Johnny O'Hanlon and Year 6

Lighting by: Mick Diver

Rehearsal help: Asma

Direction: Craig Stephens with James Yarker

P.R. by: Mobius

Stan's Cafe General Manager: Charlotte Martin

Stan's Cafe would like to thank:
The amazing staff of Billesley Primary School who have been so helpful supporting in this highly ambitious project. Especially Year 6 teachers Miss Zielinska, Mrs Leach and Miss Smith. Thanks also to the team at mac for helping us so much.

The Governing Body would like to thank:
Stan's Cafe for the wonderful partnership they have formed with the school. *Any Fool Can Start A War* is merely the most public of many projects we have created together over the last two years. The positive impact they have on the learning, expectations and experiences of our children has been wonderful and we look forward to collaborating on many more exciting adventures in the future.

Follow all the action from Billesley Primary School, including Billesley Radio podcasts at: **www.billesleyblog.com**

Follow Stan's Cafe's professional productions, international touring and home venue fun at **www.stanscafe.co.uk**, sign up to email updates via **admin@stanscafe.co.uk**

Article for Research In Drama Education

"We would like to make a show about the Cuban Missile Crisis with all 60 of your Year 6 students. We want it performed on the main stage of the local arts centre for a paying public and call it Any Fool Can Start A War"

Stan's Cafe

- If you are going to challenge others, you should probably be prepared to challenge yourselves.
- If you are going to keep yourselves vital, you should probably put yourselves into uncomfortable positions.
- If you are going to learn, you need to brave the unknown.
- If you are going to ask for someone's trust, you need to show that you trust them.
- If you are ever going to make anything happen, you should probably just say you are going to do something – and then go and do it.

Why shouldn't shows made with children take on big subjects? Why shouldn't they grapple with complex history? Why shouldn't adults and children learn together on a journey to making an ambitious work of art?

"They enjoyed their Second World War topic, so this would be a good follow on" Ms. Zielinska replied and a few months later she was on stage reading a bedtime story to her fictional daughter, Emma. This story is designed to take the daughter's mind off a possible confrontation in the school playground the following day. It is the tale of how World War 2 ended in nuclear explosions and quickly chilled to become the Cold War. This tale inevitably mutates into a crazy dream through which Emma wanders for the next hour. In a wry twist on convention Emma wakes discover her dream was true; she has just lived through the Cuban Missile Crisis.

"I loved the challenge within it, the political concepts that mean so much to me personally, I'm always talking about social justice through the curriculum at school and I'm not always sure people know what I mean - but there it was in front of me today - just a complete ideal of what I would want, there, my school and children on stage at the mac [arts centre]."

Jo Clifton, Headteacher.

Of course the key learning in this project came not through the history but the rehearsals and performance, the building of confidence and teamwork, looking people in the eye, becoming confident enough to stand up tall in front of people, speaking loud enough to be heard, being bold enough to claim the stage as yours.

The process was not easy. Learning the social skills to work together with a common goal is not an easy thing. Developing the maturity to know when you must be quiet and when you must support and when you need to speak up and ask for help is not an easy thing.

We started with simple drama exercises of walking together and stopping together, listening to each other and working as a cohesive group, aware of others around us. We asked the students to make gestures and noises. Finally we asked them to say something in front of the rest of the group. Those who were too shy to do these things were kept behind to try again in a smaller group. Those who were too shy to do even this received further attention later on. Shannon, who played JFK, came from the second group. By the time the performance arrived this fact seemed absurd.

Stan's Cafe's rules were simple:
- everyone is in the show.
- everyone speaks in the show.
- everyone has a named part.

The Student's rules were simple:
- the show needs to have songs.
- it has got to be fun.

We failed to keep to all our rules. One child, who was great in early rehearsals, was refused permission by her parents to appear on the stage. She took it well. We were heartbroken.

We kept their rules. The Americans (all girls) had a song. The Soviets (all boys) had a song. Cubans (both boys and girls) had a song. These three songs layered to become a fourth song. Everyone joined in the show's grand finale – *The Telephone Song* – the basic premise of which was, if there were more "jaw jaw" then there would be less "war war". The students helped write all the lyrics.

Of course the show had to be written bespoke for the occasion. We needed a play with sixty speaking parts tailored to the abilities and personalities of the cast. In order to allow us to create this close match we wrote nothing before we had met the classes and continued to write script between rehearsals. We created a part for Dawid so he could write and perform much of his own script in Polish. The quietest students had roles such as radar and radio operators who we would expect to hear speaking over microphones. Chloe, who was great when not directly facing an audience, could be a U2 pilot, on stage but facing the wings, her face projected large scale across the back wall via a video relay. Students who worked hard were rewarded with larger parts.

For the less confident performers 'Grandmothers Footsteps' provided a template for an invasion of the Bay of Pigs scene. The whole group devised inventive plots for 'Operation Mongoose'. A few of their plans to assassinate Castro managed to be even more outlandish than genuine CIA proposals. Everyone could help making props – paper boats, submarines and airplanes. Everyone could draw backdrops to locate the scenes – A4 pictures scanned and projected on the backdrop.

"I could keep naming individual success stories - [name redacted] who didn't talk to us a few months ago had complete ownership of his part and played it to the full."

Jo Clifton, Headteacher

Nothing happened before SATS were finished. Even then fitting in around lessons proved demanding. The staff had to be highly flexible and confident that we knew what we were doing – which we usually did. There were times when rehearsals seemed to be getting us no where, scenes which had been polished one day were totally forgotten come the next. With honourable exceptions learning lines was a slow process. Peer pressure took a while to take hold and only the looming threat of embarrassment in front of hundreds of audience members seemed to finally focus minds. Eventually, with a day or two to go, everyone was 'off book'.

Ultimately, like great sporting achievement, everything came down to confidence. The school had confidence in us, we had confidence in the students and because we had confidence in them they had to have confidence in themselves. We explained how to be embarrassed on stage is embarrassing, how having confidence in yourself breeds audience confidence in you. Relax and the show takes off.

Relentlessly we told them how good the show was, how much people would love it and how much better it would be if they displayed – even faked – confidence on the stage. They had to believe us. They had to be proud of what they were doing.

When finally students and teachers started to see all the elements of the show coming together their confidence started to grow. When Kay arrived from Birmingham Repertory Theatre with hangers full of costumes, each individually named, they realised how good they were all going to look and another surge in confidence hit. Being featured in local papers provided a further boost. When The Metro carried a photo of the show across the country and Michael Rosen picked up on this feature to endorse our project on daytime television the whole school community felt they were genuinely part of something a little special.

Ultimately it was in performance that the cast made their most impressive progress. They raised their game for the first audience and the positive response of this audience led to an improved second performance and by the third performance. The hesitancy of the opening show had transformed into something approaching boldness.

Years 2 – 5 were bussed in to see one or other of the two matinee performances, along with other teachers, support staff and parents. The final show took place on Thursday evening, parents and family were joined by genuine, ticket buying members of the public.

"I sat there watching today and just wanted to cry and I think that's why I kept laughing too because it was so powerful and so moving. The children had such ownership over some very complex ideas and could deliver them with passion"

Jo Clifton, Headteacher

Of course it was only possible to make *Any Fool Can Start A War* with Billesley Primary School because we had worked with them for the previous two years on other projects. In Autumn 2012 we ran a *City Adventure* training day with the teachers. This was designed to more fully introduce them to the school's locality – very few teachers live in the community that their students are drawn from. We also aimed to provoke staff into greater team working, greater confidence in risk taking and creative teaching. Along the way we were attempting to prove our own worth.

Also in Autumn 2012 the whole school worked with us creating a marble run that circumnavigated the school's corridors. In Spring / Summer 2013 we ran a series of week-long projects with various year groups tied into their curriculum and concluded the year by giving Sports Day the full Olympic treatment with banners, bunting, fanfares and live sporting commentary.

At the start of the next academic year we sat down with senior leaders and identified communication skills, particularly speaking, as a whole school focus. We then met with staff from each year group to learn which aspects of the year ahead they wanted our help with. It was notable that in this second year more teachers arrived with their own ideas and suggestions. For some groups this meant refining projects we had run the previous year (*The Tudors* in Year 2 and *Space* in Year 5). With others we tried new things – a *Scalextric Grand Prix* with Year 6, *Weather Poems* and *Costumes* with Year 3. *Seaside Performances* with Year 2. Each project was focused towards generating material for a school radio station which ran for a week at the end of the year and re-launched the school's blog.

"It has been amazing seeing the staff move from that initial silence and bemusement when you came to meet them to the relationship we have with you now where [...] I don't have to be involved, people just get on, plan and work together with you as the expectation at Billesley"

Jo Clifton, Headteacher

None of this success is accidental. We chose to work in conditions which would maximise our chances of success. Schools applied to work with us and Billesley offered a wonderful combination of enabling factors. As a school starting to climb out of special measures there was an enormous potential for us to make a difference. The school had physical space for us to work in (spare classrooms). Most importantly, in Jo Clifton it had (and still has) a Headteacher who understands completely the potential that the arts have to transform school life and the lives of their children, not just around the edges of their educational experience but at the heart of their learning.

"At the time [you joined us] Billesley was just beginning to come out of the darkest place possible and the work that we have done with you, that you have led, has been so powerful in shaping that ethos, in challenging us and moving us forward to the very happy place we are now."

Jo Clifton, Headteacher

The next challenge? Well, in Billesley we want to continue to push ourselves and the school. We want to keep everything fresh, exciting and ambitious. We want the school to be recognised as the outstanding learning community we feel it is. Further afield we are expanding the number of Partner Schools we are working with.

There are now two further primary schools and two secondary schools in our network. The secondary schools are more challenging environments in which to work; departmental silos, rigid timetables, greater numbers and exam performance pressures make creative working so much more challenging, but these schools too are convinced by the potential of the arts to help them and we are working hard with them to realise this potential.

Having five schools in our network introduces the potential for ideas and experiences to be shared. Last week at a breakfast meeting we sat with four Headteachers plotting a joint project that would address the government's challenge to teach Modern British Values in school. I doubt this will prove as spectacular as *Any Fool Can Start A War* but it promises to be even more challenging.

James Yarker, 14 December, 2014

About the illustration and design

The illustrations for the covers of these books were undertaken by students at Birmingham City University as the final module of their first-year illustration course during the Spring/Summer of 2018. The images were developed through workshops using variations of the theatre-devising methods employed by Stan's Cafe but adapted and applied to the making of visual work. The resulting work was shown in the pop-up exhibition *The Something Of Somebody Something* at Stan's Cafe's venue @AE Harris in May 2018.

The design concept of the books was produced by final year Graphic Design student Aimee Chapman. These were then further developed for print in a collaborative process between Stan's Cafe and the University's Innovation Product Support Service (IPSS) which involved helping the company to select appropriate DTP software, undertaking training and selecting a suitable print on demand service.

Gareth Courage
Lecturer in Illustration
Birmingham City University

www.ingramcontent.com/pod-product-compliance
Lightning Source LLC
Chambersburg PA
CBHW071757080526
44588CB00013B/2272